Just Like Me

the poetry of

Kentrell Blanche

ISBN:

978-1-105-35052-8

*And it occurs to me that
I have more in common
with the world than I
thought. We are all…*

...influenced by love

#1/Curiously, I go

Surely Heaven must see me
As some sort of fool;
I have been back and forth
Between hands-
Now,
I am here with you..
Offering the same opportunities
As I did before,
Closing my eyes to those things
That perhaps
I should not ignore..
Similar thoughts,
Similar patterns;
Questioning a future
That is perhaps too premature to matter..
Here I go again-
Giving in,
Trusting that the outcome
Will be worth the sin

I follow your shadow-
Wishing that this will last,
Fighting desperately not to
Compare you to my past..
But,
The concerns are there;
And though it may not be fair,
I find myself wondering if
It would be in my best interest
Not to care..
I can't take another tragedy
Of being left out;
Yet,
I can't help but wonder
What loving you
Is truly all about

#2/Grateful

I just wanted to take a moment
To reflect on what may appear to others
As minor components-
Your voice,
Motions of who you are;
It is your wisdom
That lifts me to greater heights by far..
I opened my hands with intentions to feel
And discovered a definition
Far more precious than <u>real</u>..
I found an all new reason to breathe
Whose passion surpasses
Every fantasy conceived..
Your presence does more than complete;
It breaks down barriers
That once prevented increase

#3/United

Treading trials of life can be hard
And sometimes we stumble;
I have seen good times
But,
There are more to be discovered..
And now that you are here,
I know that love is near..
I spread my wings and soar
Even higher;
I know that someday,
We will be just as close
As I desire..
But for now,
We are free-
Free to give in,
Free to come together,
Free to construct a foundation
Which could possibly last forever..
And once the vessel is complete,
We will be sheltered in peace;
Finally,
Our weary hearts will have relief

#4/Who you are

I could write my emotions
All through the day;
But still,
I would not have
The words to say..
My love for you
Comes without description;
You have my heart,
You have my attention..
Though the connection shared
Is from a distance,
You ease my soul
And grant my wishes..
Though I cannot feel your hand,
You are beyond being
Worth the chance-
A chance that I will take
For all of the love
There is to make..
Though I cannot touch you,
I know how I feel;
And though I have no physical
confirmation,
I know that you are real

I could fill my pages
With every word in my heart;
But still,
I could never express
My gratitude for you
Being who you are

#5/Guided by your hand

Your voice,
Your strength,
Your mind;
You graced me with your presence
Right on time...
All was uncertain
All was damaged
All was lost;
I took the high road
When I should have fought..
I was so lonely,
I was so desperate to belong,
So accustomed to my own sad song...
But then,
There was you-
Fresh and out of the blue

Like stars in a darkened sky,
You brought beauty to my life;
Blessing me with
-laughter,
-smiles
-and happy days
Because of you,
I was able to say farewell
To those spiritually taxing days
And welcome a new way of life;
A life of more
-positive thinking
-faithful walking
-optimistic conversation
-a newfound hope for relations
For you,
I am thankful
For you,
I cry
For without your embrace,
I would have never found the light

#6/Mind of a Rose

Like a rose,
You blossomed in my garden,
Contributing to the beauty
Of my ordinary hillside ever so elegantly;
True unity,
Both you and me...
In the beginning,
You were nothing more than
An uncertain seed
With much to heed...
But,
I took a chance-
Soiled my hands;
Placed you
Within the depths of my heart,
And covered you
With the warmth of my soul...
After much commitment,
You began to sprout-
Flourishing with love
Both inside and out...
I am so glad that I found the need
To give you
My devotion and time;
For now,
It is you who
Graces me with peace of mind

#7/In your favor

Falling in love again-
How exciting;
But,
Chances are
I will not survive this..
Much like the wind,
Emotions cannot be seen
But can cause damage
When challenged
Or mismanaged;
And who wants that?
Back and forth,
Around
And around
In circles;
Nothing is certain-
Not even the rising
Of the Sun
But,
I am here
With no recollection
Of all that you have done

My only focus is
My purpose
In your life;
With every memory,
Comes a price-
And for you,
I will pay
Until there is no more..
Falling in love once again-
How naïve of me;
My heart is open,
You have access
To all of my treasures;
I pray
That you will not cash in my love
For your pleasure

#8/Feel no remorse for me

I took it upon myself
To walk right through your door;
So,
Don't you feel the need to apologize
For not being the prize
That I was looking for..
With one hand,
I covered your mouth;
And with the other,
I reached for your soul;
I was anxious,
I was reckless,
I was out of control..
I kept trying
And fighting a war
That had no victory
For me-
The perfect example
Of just how foolish I can be..
The truth can sometimes
Be as cold as the snow;
All I ever wanted
Was to hold you close..
I followed you around
Like a lost breeze;
Nothing like false hope
To bring me to my knees

I have been counting my blessings
Since the day that you waved goodbye;
But,
It would have been Heaven on Earth
If you would have stayed in my life..
Goodbye, love of mine;
Thank you for your time

...torn when we must start again

#9/Departing hearts

We said
Things that
Lovers should never say;
I smiled as you walked away-
My pride led me
To keep it all in..
It was your hand
That I learned to trust;
What happened to us-
Back to square one again..
You wished me well,
I bade you the same;
And here we are:
So broken,
So black,
So far-
Apart..
I thought of calling
On you
But if you
Didn't hear my cries before,
I would only be wasting time
By reaching out to you more..
Time flies,
Welcomes unforetold goodbyes;
And sadly,
That is the story of you and I

#10/Starting with me

Finally,
I see you for who you truly are,
You and your scattered heart-
Leaving your poisons everywhere..
Who knew
That you
Would turn out the way you did;
So brittle and counterfeit-
You left me in despair..
Old love,
Don't you have anything to say to me?
How about an apology
For leading me on?
I bet you never even took the time
To consider the condition
Of this heart of mine;
Without remorse,
You are gone..
I opened my door
And let down my defenses;
You made a fool of me
But,
Nothing comes without consequences

One day,
You will feel just as I am feeling right now;
You will want to break free
But,
You won't know how..
And then,
You will see
That everything you ever wanted
Could have started
Here with me

#11/Traces

He was a rolling stone
And quietly,
I pushed him along
And made room for me;
No need in wasting time
When it comes to being free..
He would have never settled,
I saw the signs;
I witnessed the action
And read between the lines..
It would have been a storm
On timid seas;
And all of the waves
Would have rushed back to me-
Washing away all of my loveliness
And called forth excuses for my ugliness..
He was a rolling stone
And I rolled him away;
But still,
He left a trace

#12/Attachments

Though I open my heart
To make room for love,
I have learned to expect the worst
As proudly delivered
By my passionate first..
The hands
That I tend to choose
Have a way of leaving me to be confused
And lead to me sea
Where I will be sure to become
Yesterday's news..
Intentions
And promises
Do not outweigh
Actions and memories;
And oh what sour delights
Lovers blend for me-
Passion,
Neglect,
Protection,
And disrespect

A whirlwind
Of "what should have been's"
Add to my sorrow
Like dividends..
But,
Not in my favor;
It is the worst experiences
That I tend to savor..
And for years,
I have been holding on to you;
I guess that is what happens
When we lose sense
Of true

#13/Matters of the heart

I fade away
Inside and out
I lose myself
As I live without-
No phone calls,
No time spent,
No birthday cards,
No way to vent...
He just doesn't understand me,
He doesn't get it,
He is supposed to play
The role of the man
But, he just doesn't fit it..
He doesn't seem to heed
All of the things
That my tiny heart needs...
He says the words
But, words are barely good enough;
He uses the lines
But, lines won't hardly sustain my love..
And I am so tired of settling for less,
So weary from always putting
My true feelings to rest..
I need passion,
I need affection
Why must love constantly
Guide me in the wrong direction?

#14/Fall of love

Four walls
And a roof alone
Does not make a home;
We settle for less
For reasons of our own;
Who wants to be alone?
Who wants to be without?
We love wholeheartedly
But, what is love truly about?
Is it the kisses and hugs,
Late night back rubs?
The emotions we dwell in,
The arms we fell in?
We give love
In order to receive,
We tell the truth
So that we are easily believed

Love;
It comes in all shapes
And forms
And colors
And dimensions;
But, who really knows
What the hell
They should be feeling?
Emotions come and go,
Eyes begin to seek other interests
And suddenly,
Sincerity starts to fade
Starting with the words we mention..
Face to face,
Time and space;
How can one stop the love
From becoming displaced?

#15/Broken lease

No need to stress over
Breaking the lease;
I take it upon myself
To leave in peace..
You can have all that you see
For it all no longer means a thing to me..
Not even the bed,
Not even the ring;
It all has been permanently stained
With sour memories and broken dreams..
And yes,
Our time together was just
As dreadful as it seemed-
Secret faces in and out of our home;
And no,
You certainly were not alone..
I had my fixes as well;
We were characters in some
Less than satisfying fairytale..
Our union came with prices
Much too expensive to afford;
But still,
We both came aboard-
Aboard a ride not soon forgotten,
A ride that will prove to serve
As the purpose of our view on life
Becoming both spoiled and rotten

We both have our imperfections,
We both have our flaws
But, I am taking upon myself
Abandon this hopeless cause

#16/All I ever wanted

All I ever wanted was
For you to love me
Just as I love you;
Staring in your eyes alone
Makes all my dreams come true..
I rest out on the water's edge,
Just longing for the day
That you make your pledge-
To be mine alone
And promise protect my heart
As you would do your own..
I have been there during
The summer's drought
As well as the winter's cold;
For you,
I give it all-
Mind,
Body,
And soul..
I battle the circumstances
Just to overcome the hesitation
Of second chances
And unearned advances..
I could never leave you behind;
Though its blow can be deadly,
Love's embrace is one of a kind

Good times come
Then fade away,
Leaving room for misery
To come and play..
All I ever wanted was your hand,
All I ever wanted was
To wake up with you next to me;
For your love,
I offer the best of me

#17/Broken one

Am I not more than a mere tool
For your pleasure?
Am I not more than flesh and blood?
Do I not feel when I am struck?
Am I not entitled to flee
When the pain is all too much?
Am I not more than the perfect candidate
For your cheap labor?
Is the usefulness of my hands
Truly limited to carrying
The burdens of my neighbor?
I cry,
I fall,
I grieve;
And I am not just as entitled as you
To receive?
I want all of my blessings,
I want everything that is mine;
I have given off the sweat
And I have put in the time..
Am I not more
Than what you allow me to be?
If I don't stand my ground,
I will never be free

I smile when you abuse me
But, that's not right;
Because of you,
I can't sleep at night
All I ever wanted was
The opportunity to love you
And start everyday with your conversation;
But, what about my rewards?
Where is the appreciation?
Am I not more than a man?
Am I not entitled to a chance?
I could love you in different languages
Every moment that you wake;
But, how can I offer anything
When it is always me
That you forsake?

...thirsty for peace

#18/Dimensions of life

Consumed by
The superficial tunes
That we hum to-
This is what we
Have come to..
Dancing loosely
To melodies masked
By fear obtained
From tribulations
Of our past..
Sometimes,
We lose;
Sometimes,
We win;
We count our blessings
According to how we feel within..
Blue skies
In fact do not always entice the eye;
Especially when there is a storm
Ripping through our fields inside..
Laughing
And carrying on,
Holding fast to pride
Just to keep
The element of loneliness
Off of our side

Moments pass,
Memories last;
Just what do we have to do
In order to discover something
To look forward to?
Just what is there
Waiting for us?
Certainly,
There has to be
A few souls out there
Left to trust..
Deceived by faulty rhythms
That claim our children;
Life is falling apart
Even for the pure at heart

#19/Society's titles

Men in suits
Establish groups
Just to keep us less than equal;
Yesterday was slavery,
Today is the sequel..
Timid minds
Dare not stand out of line;
Tribulations never change,
Just become more clever with time..
I follow the voices
Of my fallen ancestors
Through the rubble
And the rain;
And thank God
For knowledge gained..
But,
What is knowledge
Without openness to fault?
We are all yearning for something;
But,
Dreams are seldom caught..
Simply because we seldom reach;
Most goals are certainly
More enticing to speak of
Than to keep

We follow the movement
Just to have our voices heard;
Many can go on for hours
But few truly have
A passion for the words..
Men in suits establish groups
Just to keep the war fed;
We could all be powerful together
But,
We tend to fall for the hype instead

#20/Wasting away

Almost out of gas
And my phone is going dead;
I left my wallet
At the edge of my bed..
What a day,
Patience fades away;
I don't even know where I am going
But,
There is no time to waste..
I woke up,
Fed the fish,
And got dressed;
I threw on anything,
This blue Monday doesn't deserve
To see me at my best..
Fortunes untold
Only poison my soul;
It doesn't matter where I end up
Just as long as I am whole..
No goals for today,
I just want to park;
And dwell on the burdens
That rattle my heart

Purpose in life
Depends on passions and pleasures;
Lord,
Send me a sign;
I need to get it together..
For I am wasting away,
I am wasting away

...yearning to evolve

#21/Written December 5, 2011

A timid soul
In my own little space
In such a massive world;
Cold to love and happiness-
Consumed by loneliness
And at times,
That is exactly what I prefer..
Strangers see my face
And wonder what is going on,
What has gone wrong..
I have told my story a thousand times
But,
Nothing I say seems to breach
Such clever minds..
Staring out of a dusty window
At neighbors passing by;
My seclusion keeps them
From passing in and out
Of my life..
Nothing comes easily
And I can't remember the last time-
- *Someone needed me,*
- *Someone called my name,*
- *Someone sheltered me from the rain*

I have told my story a thousand times
But,
No one ever sees me for more
Than just another sad story
With a climax of fallen glory..
And perhaps that is the very role
That I portray;
Maybe one day
I will choose the right message
And you will understand
Every word I say

#22/Crossing lines

Though I wish it could be more,
I don't want to press the issue
And lose a good thing;
Oh what unpleasant fates
Life tends to bring..
Forgive me
For thinking of you inappropriately
But with you being who you are,
How could you possibly
Expect me not to want to
Take things far-
Perhaps farther
Than they are meant to be?
So much for the dreams
That I had for you and me..
During the day,
I will still give you your time;
And though it will kill me,
I will do my best
Not to cross the line

#23/As I evolve

Is it arrogance?
Or is it growth?
I no longer feel a connection
With those whom I once cherished most..
I see their faces
And remember their names
But,
The chemistry is no longer the same..
I hear their voices
And record their words
And wonder how such foolery
Was what I once preferred..
Loose laughter over this and that;
Following crowds without
Gathering the facts..
I feel the breeze of windows left open
And feel the regret of words unspoken..
Even with my favorite pen,
I cannot rewrite habits
Lingering from back then..
Moving forward is the only prize
That I have left;
And glory be to God-
I have discovered myself

Be it arrogance,
Be it growth;
I have been there-
Done that;
And have mastered the ropes

#24/Out of reach

I have never seen so many faces
That I can't trust;
And I have never met
So many obstacles
That interfered with us..
You are so wrapped up
In the world
And consumed by opinions;
You barely pay attention
When I am expressing
My feelings..
In one ear and out of the other-
You are putting me through;
What happened to the love
That was once so true?
We are tearing down the walls
In our home;
I used to be so sure
That it was in your arms
Where I belonged

But lately,
You have been pulling back
From me
And that only leads me
To believe
That this war
No longer has a cause;
Perhaps forever
Is not forever after all
We are treading in opposite directions
Down the road
And there seems to be
No reason
To reacquaint our souls..
Maybe this love can't be saved
And perhaps we will see brighter days;
But right now,
I am lost
And freedom just seems
So far away

#25/Towards the Sun

I find myself walking
For miles at a time-
Just to keep busy,
Just to soothe my mind..
In this life,
There are blessings;
In this life,
There are rewards;
But,
What life is there
When everything
Is on a separate accord..
There is growth
And prosperity
For all of those around me;
But,
When will my trumpets
Be sounded?
When will I know
All that I need to know?
When will my blood
Once again
Begin to flow?

It seems that I am following
In the footsteps
That I have already made;
Surely by now,
I should have been saved..
My day
Has to be on its way;
Until then,
I have to keep on smiling-
Keep on looking
Towards the Sun

You can't stand above if you can't stand alone

-Kentrell Blanche

This book was inspired by a new face to my life.
He alone has unveiled to me the truth that love is
not yet lost. Though his identity will go unknown,
his name echoes in my heart.

Forever,
Kentrell

www.ingramcontent.com/pod-product-compliance
Lightning Source LLC
Chambersburg PA
CBHW020525030426
42337CB00011B/543